What Does a
Saw Do?

by Robin Nelson

Lerner Publications Company · Minneapolis

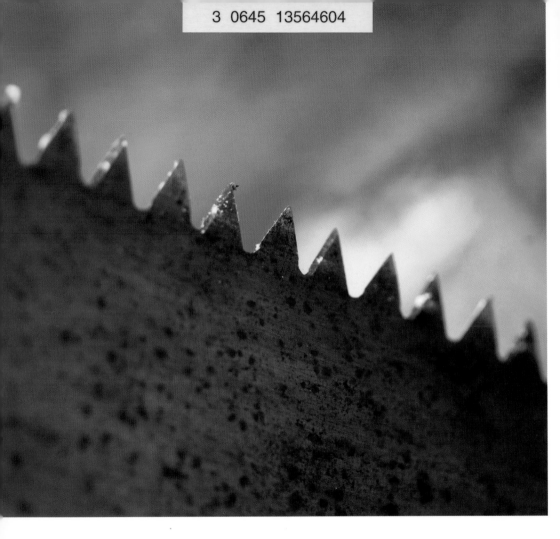

What tool is this?

It is a saw.

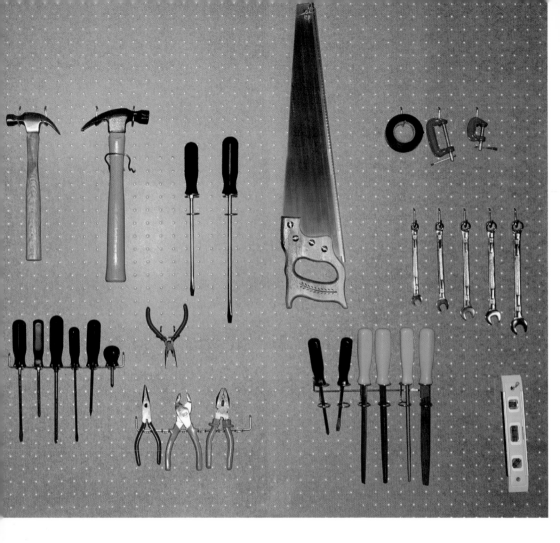

Tools help us do jobs.

Saws make jobs easier.

Saws cut wood.

There are many different kinds of saws.

This is the **blade** of a handsaw.

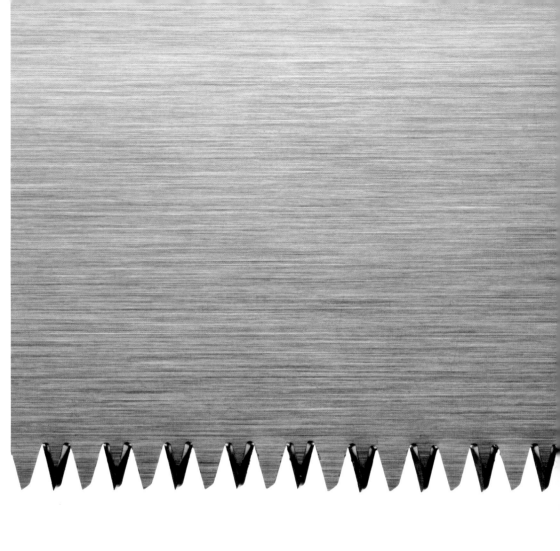

The blade is made of **steel**.

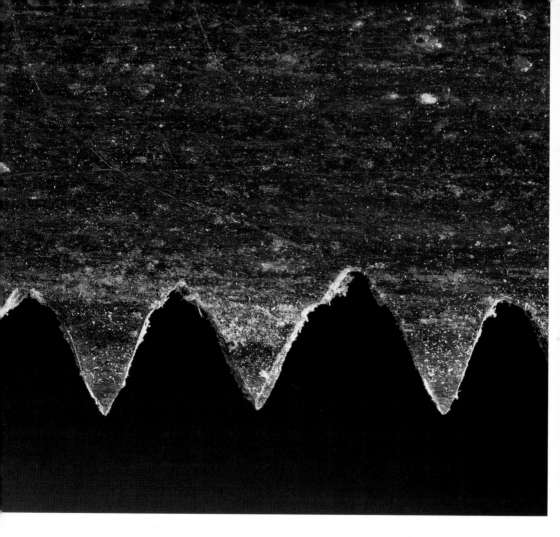

The blade has many **teeth**.

The teeth are very sharp.

This is the saw's handle.

We hold the handle. We push and pull the saw across the wood.

13

A **carpenter** works with a saw.

Builders use saws to cut
wood for houses.

You can use a saw to
build a birdhouse.

What other jobs can you
do with a saw?

Saws Are Wedges

Saws are simple machines. They are **wedges**. A wedge is shaped like a triangle. Wedges are often used to cut or split things.

Hold on to a saw's handle. Touch the blade to a piece of wood. Press down and slowly push the saw away from your body. The saw acts as a wedge. It splits the wood.

Safety First

 Ask a grown-up to help before using any tools.

 Wear safety glasses to protect your eyes.

 Roll up your sleeves. Tuck in your shirt. Tie back your hair. Remove any jewelry that might get in the way.

 Carry a saw with the blade down and away from your body.

Never run with a tool in your hand.

 Keep your fingers away from the blade when you are cutting wood.

 Never touch the saw's teeth.

 Put away the saw when you are done with your job.

Glossary

 blade – the flat, sharp part of a tool used for cutting

 carpenter – a person who builds things out of wood

 steel – a strong, hard metal

 teeth – sharp points that stick out of a tool

 wedges – objects shaped like a triangle that are used to split things

Index

LERNER

SOURCE

Expand learning beyond the printed book. Download free, complementary educational resources for this book from our website, www.lerneresource.com.

The images in this book are used with the permission of: © Jean Schweitzer/Dreamstime.com, p. 2; © Mark Humphreys/Dreamstime.com, p. 3; © Thinkstock Images/Comstock Images/Getty Images, p. 4; © Kim D. French/Shutterstock.com, p. 5; © Jupiterimages/Workbook Stock/Getty Images, p. 6; © iStockphoto.com/val_th, p. 7; © iStockphoto.com/Gennady Kravetsky, pp. 8, 22; © iStockphoto.com/DNY59, pp. 9, 22; © iStockphoto.com/Koczina Balázs, pp. 10, 22; © Wavebreakmedia Ltd/Dreamstime.com, p. 11; © Tuja66/Dreamstime.com, p. 12; © Dorling Kindersley/the Agency Collection/Getty Images, p. 13; © Johner/Johner Images/Getty Images, pp. 14, 22; © Terje Rakke/Riser/Getty Images, p. 15; © Jeff Schultz/Glow Images, p. 16; © Jose Luis Pelaez Inc/Blend Images/Getty Images, p. 17; © Laura Westlund/Independent Picture Service, pp. 18, 20, 21, 22.

Front cover: © donatas1205/Shutterstock.com.

Main body text set in ITC Avant Garde Gothic Std Medium 21/25.
Typeface provided by Adobe Systems.

Lerner Publications Company
A division of Lerner Publishing Group, Inc.
241 First Avenue North
Minneapolis, MN 55401 U.S.A.

Website address: www.lernerbooks.com

Library of Congress Cataloging-in-Publication Data

Nelson, Robin, 1971–
    What does a saw do? / by Robin Nelson.
      p.   cm. — (First step nonfiction–tools at work)
    Includes index.
    ISBN 978–0–7613–8979–8 (lib. bdg. : alk. paper)
    1. Saws—Juvenile literature. I. Title.
    TJ1235.N45 2013
    621.9′34—dc23   2011039076

Manufactured in the United States of America
1 – BC – 7/15/12